W0231581

Chris Oyakhilome, D.Sc., D.D

Don't Stop Here!

A Spiritual Journey to Greater Impact

LoveWorld Publishing

Don't Stop Here!...*a spiritual journey to greater impact*

ISBN 978-37061-5-2

First Printing 2004

All scripture quotations are taken from the King James Version of the Bible unless otherwise indicated.

Published by: LoveWorld Publishing
3, Adebayo Akande Street, Oregun, Ikeja, Lagos, Nigeria.
Email: info@loveworldbooks.org
Website: www.loveworldbooks.org

UNITED KINGDOM:
Believers' LoveWorld
Unit C2, Thames view
Business center
Barlow way, Rainham
Essex, RM 13 8BT
Tel: +44 (0) 170 855 6604

USA:
Christ Embassy Houston
8623 Hemlock Hill Drive
Houston Texas 77083
Tel: +1 281 759 5111;
+1 281 759 6218

CANADA:
600 Clayson Road,
North York Toronto M9M 2H2
Canada
Tel/Fax:+1-416-746 5080

NIGERIA:
Christ Embassy
Plot 97, Durumi District,
Abuja, Nigeria.

LoveWorld Conference Center
Kudirat Abiola Way, Oregun
P.O. Box 13563 Ikeja, Lagos.
Tel:+234-808 586 5700,
+234-817 198 7339
+234-802 478 9892-3

SOUTH AFRICA:
303 Pretoria Avenue
Cnr. Harley and Bram Fischer
Randburg, Gauteng
South Africa
Tel: +27 11 3260971
+27 11 3260972

email: info@loveworldbooks.org
website: www.loveworldbooks.org

Contents

Introduction

Ignorance of God's Word is a destroyer. God said,

> **"My people are destroyed** (that is, they perish, suffer, are brought down and crushed) **for lack of knowledge..." (Hosea 4:6).**

In other words, they are impoverished, punished, brought down, crushed and destroyed because they lack knowledge - spiritual knowledge. They get into trouble for their lack of knowledge (Isaiah 5:13).

I can't understand a Christian who

wants to grow in the things of God but doesn't invest in spiritual things. Some Christians have a library of worldly home videos; they can be described as 'champions in worldly video collections.' If you're that way, you're known in Heaven as a carnal Christian; and if you want to see the glory of God in your life, then you must put a stop to it. You've got to change. You can't keep collecting such things and still expect to grow in God.

Remember that your life is the character of the things you watch, read and listen to. Make no mistakes about it; what you are today is an expression of what you put into you yesterday! Your life today is therefore the result of the things you've been feeding your inner man on.

The Most Important Thing In Your Life

By the time you're through reading this book, something should have happened in your life. There should be changes; there should be results; there should be transformations. You should have made spiritual progress. Don't merely lend mental assent to everything you read and say, "Oh yeah, I've heard all this before..." Make up your mind for a change right now before you read any further!

If you want gold you must dig for it. You don't find gold anywhere on the top soil; you'll have to dig deep to strike gold. If you really want spiritual progress, you must prepare for it. You'll need to change the things you read, watch and listen to! You'll need to increase your desire for fellowship with the Spirit and with God's people. It's like telling a student, "If you don't go to class and you don't study, you'll fail your exams." That's a very simple, yet very powerful principle. Now, we're not talking about exams in school, but exams in life. To have a 'D' in any course in school is bad but having a 'D' in life is terrible. You may flunk your exams in school and still make it through life, but if you flunk life's exams, you're sunk!

God is concerned about your spiritual growth. He wants you to make progress spiritually. He wants your language and daily communication to conform with His Word only. He wants you to increase in spiritual knowledge and understanding. That's why you have this book in your hands right now; it's not a chance occurrence. God wants you to grow by virtue of the information you're about to receive from this book.

The time is short; there's no time to play around. What would you say you've done for the Lord with your life? What would you say is the most important thing to you in your life? I'll help you answer that: **What you spend most of your time on, what you give the most attention to, what you spend the most of your money on – whether or not you realize it - is the most important thing in your life.**

You know, sometimes, people say, "God is the most important One in my life." But how much time do they spend with Him? Little wonder Jesus said in Matthew 7:22-23, **"Many will say to me in that day, Lord, Lord, have we not prophesied in thy**

name? and in thy name have cast out devils? and in thy name done many wonderful works? And then will I profess unto them, I never knew you..." This is because they never had fellowship with Him.

Are you still unknown to the Lord and His holy angels? Are you still in the shadows after one year of being born-again? What kind of life are you living? Is your impact being felt where you are? Have you found your place? Have you found something you can identify with?

I believe there's a place for everybody. If you're winning souls and leading people to Christ, there's no way, sooner than later, that others wouldn't take notice of you. That's because people will have testimonies of how you led them to

Christ; of how they came to church because you invited them, and before long, you'll be out of the shadows.

You need to understand that you must be known in the house of the Lord. There's no secret life in the house of God. It's not possible and it's totally unacceptable to be a secret Christian. You can't hide and say, "Well, nobody knows me but I'm very effective." If you're really effective, you'll be in the limelight, because Jesus said,

> **"No man, when he hath lighted a candle, covereth it with a vessel, or putteth it under a bed; but setteth it on a candlestick, that they which enter in may see the light" (Luke 8:16).**

What are your responsibilities in the local assembly where you belong? What do you do? What are you known for? What have you become proficient at in all your years of being a Christian?

Get Ready To Move From Gilgal To Jordan!

This book will help you find your place. It will stir you up to desire spiritual growth, move you out of your comfort zone and launch you into the deep in the realm of the Spirit. It will open your eyes to see where you are in your spiritual journey, point you in the direction you ought to be headed and show you how to get there.

The story of the journey Elijah and Elisha took from Gilgal to Jordan is very significant. It typifies the various stages of our spiritual growth and the different points we find ourselves in our walk with the Lord. Through this beautiful portion of Scripture, I'll show what each of these places Elijah and Elisha went to signifies and what you must do to move from one point to the other.

Don't stop now in your walk with God; get ready to move from Gilgal to Jordan!

— **Pastor Chris Oyakhilome**

GILGAL: 1
The Place of Beginning

"And it came to pass, when the Lord would take up Elijah into heaven by a whirlwind, that Elijah went with Elisha from Gilgal. And Elijah said unto Elisha, Tarry here, I pray thee; for the Lord hath sent me to Beth-el. And Elisha said unto him, As the Lord liveth, and as thy soul liveth, I will not leave thee. So they went down to Beth-el" (2 Kings 2:2).

I want you to note the words 'from Gilgal.' Elijah and Elisha had been at Gilgal; that was where they began their journey. Elisha had been with Elijah and had served him for long (2 Kings 3:11). Now it got to the point where the Lord was about to take Elijah home to heaven and Elijah wasn't sure Elisha was aware of it. So he said to him, "The Lord has sent me to Bethel, so you stay here at Gilgal. Don't worry about coming with me anymore. I'll continue on my own from here."

Elisha replied, "No sir! I won't. Wherever you go, I go!" So they went on together to Bethel.

Elisha was a man who knew how to press into spiritual things. His boss, Elijah, said to him, "Thank you; you've done a lot for me already. Now stop here, for the Lord has sent me to Bethel." Remember, they had been together at Gilgal. Elisha must have thought to himself: If the Lord has sent you to Bethel and the same Lord asked me to follow you, then what will I be doing here while you go on to Bethel? So he refused to stop at Gilgal and followed him on to Bethel. He continued with Elijah through the journey.

You see, this story here means a lot and you'll need to understand the significance of each of the places they journeyed to for you to get what the Spirit is communicating through this beautiful portion of the Bible.

Gilgal: The Place of Beginning

Gilgal signifies the place of beginning. It is the starting point for the new life. The word 'Gilgal' actually means, 'rolling away.' It signifies God beginning a new thing in your life, as the old one is rolled away.

"And the LORD said unto Joshua, This day have I rolled away the reproach of Egypt from off you. Wherefore the name of the place is called Gilgal unto this day"(Joshua 5:9).

The Lord called the place 'Gilgal,' because that was where He rolled away the reproach of Egypt from His people, Israel. Egypt is a type of the world, and when you come to Christ, the reproach of the world is rolled away from your life. It's the place of beginning, and the Bible tells us that God sent Elijah on His journey from there.

Elijah was about to go to heaven, but he had a ministry to fulfill in Bethel that day.

So he said to Elisha, "You stop here at the point of beginning; I'm going on to Bethel"

When you come to Christ, you're at the point of beginning - at Gigal; but don't remain there, you must move further in your life.

The Starting Point of The New Life

Gilgal represents the starting point for the babe in Christ. It's the point of salvation when you proclaim Jesus as Lord of your life. It's the point at which the Holy Spirit baptizes you into the body of Christ, but you must not remain at this point. Yes, it's true you've just come out of Egypt (the world), and its reproach has been rolled off your life now. You should thank God for that, but is that the greatest testimony of your life presently? Is that all that you can share with others about this new life you've received?

The testimony of our salvation is an eternal one, but if that's all you're going from place to place to share, it's not good enough. You've got to move forward in your life!

Several years ago, we used to sing that old song:

'I am happy, I am saved.
I am saved, I am saved.
I am happy, I am saved.
Hallelujah!'

It's a beautiful song, you ought to be glad that you're saved, but don't stop there at the point of salvation. You need to ask yourself, "Am I still tarrying at Gilgal? If Jesus comes today, will He meet me at Gilgal? Remember, Gilgal is the place of beginning;

it's not the greatest place. At Gilgal, Elijah said, "The Lord has asked me to go to Bethel," so don't stay at Gilgal, don't let Jesus meet you there! He wants you to move on.

GILGAL: THE PLACE OF RENEWAL

Gilgal is also the place of renewal. There are people who will have to start again because they had backslidden and turned to the world. When they return, they will have to go back to Gilgal. They don't just come back and continue from where they left off, they'll have to go back to Gilgal and start all over again. This is one good reason you must not waste your time doing the wrong things. You can't afford to toy with your salvation and play games with the Holy Ghost; you can never deceive Him.

1 Samuel 11:14-15 tells us something about the renewal that takes place at Gilgal:

"Then said Samuel to the people, Come, and let us go to Gilgal, and renew the kingdom there. And all the people went to Gilgal; and there they made Saul king before the Lord in Gilgal; and there they sacrificed sacrifices of peace offerings before the Lord; and there Saul and all the men of Israel rejoiced greatly"

They made Saul king at Gilgal. What does this signify? Remember that Gilgal typifies the place of the baby Christian, the spiritually immature. It is the place of carnality, and there, you tend to make the wrong choices. The children of Israel made Saul king, but Saul represents the king of the flesh. He represents the 'head-and-shoulders' government. Remember the Bible says he was head and shoulders above everybody else in Israel (1 Samuel 9:2). At Gilgal, you are inclined to choose the flesh instead of the spirit. Yet the Kingdom was being renewed while they were there.

God said He was going to give them a king, but not one according to the flesh. He had another king in mind, but they didn't know it! He said, "Behold a king shall reign in righteousness..." (Isaiah 32:1) but He was talking of the Son of God, the Lord Jesus Christ. Instead, the devil moved in on the people first, and they clamoured, "Give us a king to reign over us!"

Samuel tried to dissuade them from making such demands of God. "The Lord God is your king," he told them.

"No, we want to be like other nations!" the people retorted.

Have you ever in your life found yourself where you wanted to be like other nations? You wanted to be like your colleagues at work who didn't know God. You were asking yourself, "What do I do with my Sundays? I just go to church and spend practically the whole day there when my mates stay at home to watch matinees and home videos with their families, or go visiting with friends." Those are people of the world. Why do you let their values influence you? You ask for a renewal, but your renewal can only produce a 'king Saul' in your life!

You must therefore move on to Bethel; you cannot remain at Gilgal! Samuel knew what he was doing when he told the people to go to Gilgal and renew the kingdom there. There, Saul was made the king, because he was head and shoulders above everyone else. He was the wrong choice but that was what they asked for. What have you asked for in your life? Are you still a man or woman of the flesh who makes carnal choices? Do you still desire to be like the other nations? Are you still being influenced by men and women of the world? Do the actors and actresses of this world still inspire you? Are they your role-models?

Every one of us, somewhere down the line, has someone who motivates or inspires us. We have someone we admire in one thing or the other. I wonder who your own role-models are. Who do you aspire to be like? Who are you patterning your life after?

If they're men and women of the world, then you're still at Gilgal.

It's time for you to move on to Bethel. In the next chapter we will be looking at what Bethel signifies.

2

BETHEL: The Place of The Altar

"And the Lord appeared unto Abram, and said, Unto thy seed will I give this land: and there builded he an altar unto the Lord, who appeared unto him. And he removed from thence unto a mountain on the east of Bethel, and pitched his tent, having Bethel on the west, and Hai

on the east: and there he builded an altar unto the Lord, and called upon the name of the Lord" (Genesis 12:7-8).

Bethel is a special place. There was where Abram pitched his tent and built an altar unto the Lord. Chapter thirteen of the same book, from verse one, reads thus:

"And Abram went up out of Egypt, he, and his wife, and all that he had, and Lot with him, into the south. And Abram was very rich in cattle, in silver, and in gold. And he went on his journeys from the south even to Bethel, unto the place where his tent had been at the beginning (we read that in Genesis 12:8)**, between Bethel and Hai; Unto the place of the altar, which he had made there at the first:**

and there Abram called on the name of the Lord." (Genesis 13:1-4).

This lets us know Bethel is the place of the altar. It's the place of commitment; the place of the vow. Bethel is that place where you get to and say, "Lord, all I have is yours." It's the place where you erect an altar before the Lord. That altar in itself signifies surrender. So Bethel is also the place of surrender. Have you come to Bethel in your Christian walk?

The Place of Commitment And of The Vow

Abraham raised an altar and called upon the name of the Lord in Bethel, but his grandson, Jacob also journeyed to Bethel and there's a lot we can learn from his experience there.

"And Jacob went out from Beer-sheba, and went toward Haran. And he lighted upon a certain place, and tarried there all night, because the sun was set; and he took of the stones of that place, and put them for his pillows, and lay down in that place to sleep And he dreamed, and behold a ladder set up on the earth, and the top of it reached to heaven: and behold the angels of God ascending and descending on it. And, behold, the Lord stood above it, and said, I am the Lord God of Abraham thy father, and the God of Isaac: the land whereon thou liest, to thee will I give it, and to thy seed; And thy seed shall be as the dust of the earth, and thou shalt spread

abroad to the west, and to the east, and to the north, and to the south: and in thee and in thy seed shall all the families of the earth be blessed. And, behold, I am with thee, and will keep thee in all places whither thou goest, and will bring thee again into this land; for I will not leave thee, until I have done that which I have spoken to thee of. And Jacob awaked out of his sleep, and he said, Surely the Lord is in this place; and I knew it not. And he was afraid, and said, How dreadful is this place! this is none other but THE HOUSE OF GOD, and this is the gate of heaven. And Jacob rose up early in the morning, and took the stone that he had put for his pillows, and set it up

for a pillar, and poured oil upon the top of it. And he called the name of that place Bethel: but the name of that city was called Luz at the first. And Jacob vowed a vow, saying, If God will be with me, and will keep me in this way that I go, and will give me bread to eat, and raiment to put on, So that I come again to my father's house in peace; then shall the Lord be my God: And this stone, which I have set for a pillar, shall be God's house: and of all that thou shalt give me I will surely give the tenth unto thee" (Genesis 28:12-22).

Jacob made his commitment to God at Bethel, and said, "Lord, everything I have is yours. You, Lord, will be My God, and of all that You give me, I will surely give the tithe of it." The tithe is one-tenth of what God blesses you with. Jacob made a commitment to Jehovah at Bethel to give Him the tithe always.

Have you come to that point in your life where you know what it is to make a commitment to God? Have you made a vow to God about your life? Let me tell you something: God deals with vows; they are sacred things to Him. That's why it's important that you learn to strike a deal with God through your vows. Sometimes you may find yourself in a predicament in your life, or things are not just going right for you. That's the best time to strike a deal with God and make a vow! That way, you're challenging God to move in a certain direction for your good and you too will move in a certain direction. God can always be trusted to keep His part of the vow, but He'll watch out for you to fulfill yours.

Jacob made a vow at Bethel. He said to God, "If You would keep me in this way that I go, and give me bread to eat, and clothes to put on, and cause me to return to my father's house again in peace, then You shall be my God, and this stone that I have used as a pillow shall be an altar set up unto God."

Commit Yourself To God At Bethel

The first thing you do in Bethel is to recognize God as your Lord and commit yourself to Him. The next thing is to commit yourself to His house. When you commit yourself to God, you must also commit yourself to His house. Look at David; he said, "The Lord my God has said He would dwell in tents, but I've decided to build Him a house. How can I be in a palace and my God has no place. Surely, I will build Him a house!" (1 Chronicles 17:1).

That's the kind of commitment you show toward God and His House when you get to Bethel.

What have you done for the Lord in your life? He has given you bread to eat, clothes to put on and a place to stay, but has He become your God? If He is your God, you'll consult with Him; you'll yield yourself to Him. If He is your God, He would have the right of way in your life. We are in a generation that does not recognize God. Only the Holy Spirit can open a man's eyes to know God in this generation we live in.

It's worse than the very generation that Jesus called an evil and adulterous generation (Matthew 12:9). This is why you must be able to answer the next question clearly, without a shadow of doubt. Have you come to know Him as your God? Is He your God in this godless, heathenistic society?

Have you made your commitment to Him? Have you come to Bethel, or are you still at Gilgal where you want to be like other nations and be renewed unto Saul's rulership? The children of Israel made Saul king, but Saul represents the king of the flesh. Is that what you want for your life? Some people have been born again for ten, fifteen, maybe even twenty years, but cannot be distinguished from the new convert. What are you waiting for? Why are you still at Gilgal? You've been born again this long, but how many people have you led to Christ? You may not feel like you're ready for it, but you're going to move out of Gilgal by the anointing of the Holy Ghost! That's why you're reading this book!

Recognize that God needs you. There's a harvest of souls all over the world. Don't just sit down there with your hands folded in your laps; get up and do something!

MOVE ON FROM BETHEL!

God wants you to leave Gilgal for Bethel, but He doesn't want you to stay in Bethel either. You must move from Bethel! Consider the story of Elijah and Elisha which we're studying. Elisha went with Elijah from Gilgal to Bethel, but he didn't stop there. Elijah insisted that he stopped there but

Elisha didn't. He moved on with him to the next point. He was, in other words, telling Elijah, "Oh no, I can't stop at Bethel. I can't just make a commitment to God and stop."

Some people are just happy to stop at Bethel. They make a commitment to God; they make a vow and say, "My life is now for God." That's where some Christians are today. They're very committed, but there's a difference between faithfulness and faith. They are faithful, they can be trusted that every time the church doors open, they'll be there. Whenever there's a call for evangelism, they'll be there. Anything you tell them to do, they'll do willingly. If you tell them to go five miles, they'll go five miles, but that's just about how far they'll go.

Elijah said to Elisha, "Stop at Bethel.

That's just like some people say, "Okay, you're now committed, what else are you looking for?" Child of God, there's a place beyond Bethel; there's something more than your declaration of commitment to God; there's a Jericho to move on to!

JERICHO: 3

Where You Meet The Holy Ghost

"And Elijah said unto him, Elisha, tarry here, I pray thee; for the Lord hath sent me to Jericho. And he said, As the Lord liveth, and as thy soul liveth, I will not leave thee. So they came to Jericho" (2 Kings 2:4).

Jericho is the place where you meet the Holy Ghost. You'll find this in **Joshua 5:13-15:**

"And it came to pass, when Joshua was by Jericho, that he lifted up his eyes and looked, and, behold, there stood a man over against him with his sword drawn in his hand: and Joshua went unto him, and said unto him, Art thou for us, or for our adversaries? And he said, Nay; but as captain of the host of the Lord am I now come. And Joshua fell on his face to the earth, and did worship, and said unto him, What saith my lord unto his servant? And the captain of the Lord's host said unto Joshua, Loose thy shoe from off thy foot; for the place whereon thou standest is holy. And Joshua did so."

The man, Joshua, had not known the Holy Ghost. He was preparing to take

Jericho when he saw a man with his sword drawn, ready for a fight. Joshua fearlessly approached him and asked, "Are you for us or for our adversaries?"

"Neither of you," the Man replied, "I'm the Captain of the Lord's host."

Suddenly Joshua's eyes opened and he realized he was talking to the Holy Ghost. At this, he fell down and worshipped Him and asked, "What does my LORD have to say?"

When you come to Jericho, it means you've moved from Gilgal, where you started out, to Bethel, where you made your commitment to God. Since you didn't want to stop there, you took further steps to meet and know the Holy Ghost. Why? You have a greater work to do; there's a 'Jericho' for you to conquer and possess. There are walls that must come down, walls that must give way.

At Jericho, you meet the Holy Ghost and He changes your life as He did Joshua's. He said to Joshua, "Look, that sword you have in your hand is not going to work. You can't stand by the gates of Jericho and hope that someday they'll open up for you to rush in. You can't hope to climb the walls either. Let Me tell you what to do..."

The importance of the Holy Spirit in the things we do cannot be over emphasized. No matter what you do in God's house, whether you clean the louvers or you're the pastor, God will not bless it except it is done by the power of the Holy Spirit. According to the Bible, if it's not done by the power of the Holy Spirit, it's nothing to God. But if it is, then it is recorded in

Heaven. Even if you're cleaning the church floor, you must clean by the power of the Holy Spirit, for nothing is acceptable to God except it is presented to Him through the Holy Spirit. Jesus presented Himself as a sacrifice through the eternal Spirit, **"How much more shall the blood of Christ, who through the eternal Spirit offered himself without spot to God, purge your conscience from dead works to serve the living God?" (Hebrews 9:14).**

You see, Jericho is the place where you leave your human strategies and take up the Holy Ghost's strategies. It's the place where you stop thinking carnally, where you stop using the calculator to tell how much you can have. jericho is the place where you stop using your bank account to determine how much you're able to do. Jericho is the place where you take the Holy Ghost's strategies and use them for His glory.

The Holy Ghost said to Joshua, "Here's what you're going to do: Go round the walls, once every day for seven days. On the seventh day, go around it seven times. Be quiet all the time until the last time of the seventh day. At the last time, shout, and the walls will come down! This is another revelation in Jericho.

The Power of Praise and Silence

You realize the power of praise in Jericho. You also learn the power of silence in Jericho. When you come to Jericho, you know when to be quiet and when to shout. In Jericho, something unique happens in your life: you're at once a quiet and a shouting person. Some people look at you and say, "He's a very quiet fellow," others say, "Get to hear him when he's in church!"

In Jericho, you have the strategies of the Holy Ghost for victory in your life. You operate in the power of the Holy Ghost because you have come to know Him and His presence with you. He said to Joshua, "I am with you." When you know Him, no walls are too thick anymore. When I hear a brother or sister talk about needing a breakthrough, I know they haven't yet arrived at Jericho.

In Jericho you realize you don't need to puncture a hole through any wall in your life, you don't even need to break through it. Walls represent obstacles, barriers, challenges that separate you from God's best for you. It could be in your finances, your health, family or job. When you understand the Holy Ghost Who Joshua met at Jericho, your life will be different. You'll not be thinking of breaking through, but of the whole wall coming down. The wall will of necessity come down! Whatever barrier or challenges; whether man-made, devil-made or self-constructed; the Holy Spirit, your Helper will teach you what to do to bring them crumbling down.

Now that you have moved from Gilgal, through Bethel to Jericho, and have come to know the Holy Ghost, nothing is too hard anymore!

YOU BECOME A WARRIOR IN JERICHO!

You know, it's one thing to know how to read your Bible, pray everyday and go to church when you should, but it's another thing to live a victorious life. It's one thing to be militant in your spirit but another thing entirely to understand the battle and be victorious in it. When you say, "The battle is the Lord's," there's a lot more to it than that. It's the Lord's battle alright, but He calls you His battle axe and weapons of war (Jeremiah 51:20).

In Jericho, God doesn't command us to stand still. We don't stand still; the generation that stood still has died. Moses said to that generation, "Hey, stand still and see the salvation of God" (Exodus 14:13) - because they had the slave mentality - but remember, God's response was an urgent "Go forward!" Now, this is not the generation with the slave mentality; this new generation has the warrior mentality. We're God's gladiators, and He continually urges us to go forward and launch the offensive against the enemy.

In this new generation, not only are we militant in our spirits, we also never take 'No' for an answer or back down for the devil or give anything up to him. When you get to this point you, won't say, "The battle is the Lord's" and fold your hands. You are His battle-axe and weapons of war! He's carrying out His acts through you.

In Jericho, you pray with understanding. Now, there's a difference between praying with understanding and praying with THE understanding. Praying with the understanding means praying through your mind in a language that you understand. Praying with understanding, however, means that even though you may not be praying in the language you understand, you understand and are applying the principles of prayer; you know who you are and who God is. You understand that you're praying as a joint-heir with Christ; that means you're praying with reverence and with faith, through the Word of God. That's what it means to pray with understanding. Some people pray without understanding, so when they talk to God, He doesn't hear them and they get no results.

You've got to manifestly understand who you are and who God is, and that without faith you cannot please Him. Without the principles of God's Word in operation, your prayers are empty, even when you're praying in other tongues. Pray with your spirit open for God to hear you, and you to hear Him. That's the fellowship of the Spirit – you're talking to God and He's talking to you. It's not a one-way communication. You're pouring your heart out to Him and He's pouring His heart to you. That's fellowship, and when you fellowship with God this way through His Spirit, you're filled with wisdom and with the Word of God and you become an effective soldier in the Kingdom of God.

When you come to Jericho, you become a warrior. You see, at Gilgal, you're excited about being born again, and that's wonderful. At Bethel, you become committed to the things of God. That's great too. But when you arrive at Jericho, you become a fighter. You start talking differently. You start talking about taking cities, nations and the world. You're different now, your life has changed. You have arrived in Jericho - the place of warfare. Even your intercessory prayers have changed. Now you speak words of power; fire comes out of your mouth and you're conquering cities and nations for Jesus Christ.

I congratulate you if you're already in Jericho. If not, get out of Gilgal! Move on from Bethel! Come over to Jericho, and become a combatant for Christ. Glory to God!

JORDAN: 4
The Place of Confirmation

"And Elijah said unto him, Tarry, I pray thee, here; for the Lord hath sent me to Jordan. And he said, As the Lord liveth, and as thy soul liveth, I will not leave thee. And they two went on" (2 Kings 2:6).

At Jericho, Elijah said to Elisha again, "Stay here, for the Lord has sent me to Jordan."

Elisha said, "You mean we're not through yet? Well, I'm not through if you're not through. If the Lord has sent you to Jordan, that's where I'm going too!"

If you've been a Christian for some time – a few years, and your life hasn't caught the fire of the Spirit, then you still have a long way to go. By now your life should be on fire for God. By now there should be some fire inside you! If you're still being counselled or you still say things like, "The pastor offended me, so I'm not going to that church anymore;" if you still take offense and harbour bitterness, you're still at Gilgal, you've not even got to Bethel!

What are you waiting for when you should be winning cities and nations for Christ?

Don't stay at Gilgal; don't stop at Bethel; move on to Jericho! But something more happens when you get to Jericho. The

Voice speaks and says to you, "Move from here! I've got something for you in Jordan. Get out of Jericho, move to Jordan!"

Jordan signifies the place of confirmation. By the time you get to Jordan, you will hear a Voice from heaven saying, "This is My beloved Son in whom I am well pleased" (Matthew 3:17). This is what happened to Jesus at Jordan as He was being baptized. God spoke out from heaven and declared openly that Jesus is His beloved Son; the One in whom He was well pleased, glory, Hallelujah! As a Christian, you must come to the point in your life where that Voice of God confirms you; this takes place when you get to Jordan.

Hearing The Voice of God

There are Christians who fail to recognise God's voice. They say, "Well, I believe God talks to people but I can't say that He has spoken to me specifically." You should be ashamed to say that, because God talks every time, and if you don't know that He has spoken to you, it's because you've not been listening.

Don't say God has never spoken to you. He has spoken to you several times; you are the one who has refused to recognize His voice. When you trust in your own voice and the voices of men, God's voice wouldn't mean anything to you anymore. But God has said, "My sheep know My voice. A stranger's voice they will not follow, for they refuse to heed the voice of strangers." If I ask you whether you have heard the voice of God in the last one week, I wonder what your answer will be. God talks to you all the time. If you will listen to Him, you will hear Him and you will never dash your foot against a stone. When you hear God's voice and hearken to Him, He will fix your life and make it worth living; your life will go in the right course.

The Place of Translation

Jordan is where every trace of the old life is removed from you and the new life gains the ascendancy. It's the place where the flesh drops and the spirit takes over. The flesh can't hold you anymore; habits of the past can't stop you anymore when you get to Jordan. You know, you can be in Jericho as a warrior and still have trouble with habits trying to destroy your life. You may be in Jericho with little foxes spoiling the vine of your life. They may be there with you in Jericho, but when you get to Jordan, you're separated from them.

At Jordan, Elisha saw Elijah taken up into heaven. This means Jordan is also the place of translation. It's the place where you leave the flesh behind; it's the place where the flesh (your senses) can't hold you down anymore. The things of this life can't get a hold of you because you've soared high in the realm of the spirit. You're like Elijah and Enoch now; you now possess translational power and have been propelled into the realms of the Holy Ghost.

In Jordan, the inhabitants do not say, "I am sick." They do not say, "I am broke." There, they've learnt to live beyond their pockets and their accounts. They've learnt to live beyond the senses. They've learnt to live beyond the human body. In Jordan, you live by the power of the 'Whirlwind' – the Holy Ghost – Who transports you from the natural realm into the supernatural!

The Place of Adoption

This is what happens in Jordan. It's another kind of life in Jordan. There, you realize you have moved to the place of adoption. When God said of Jesus, "This is My beloved Son..." that was not the day Jesus became God's Son, but the day He was adopted. Adoption in the New Testament refers to the enthronement of a son. It signifies that the son has come of age. It means he can now be trusted with authority.

In all the thirty years Jesus lived on

earth before His ministry began, He didn't minister with the anointing that He had. When the time came, God said, "Now, this is My adopted Son. He has come into the place of authority. He has grown to maturity." The next thing God said was very profound; He said, "Hear ye Him!" (Matthew 17:5). Jesus had now become a man of authority; He was God's adopted Son.

> **"The earnest expectation of the creation waits for the manifestation of the *sons* of God" (Romans 8:19).**

In other words, all of creation is waiting, not for the 'children' of God, not for those who were born of Him, but for those who have been raised up and trained by God. They're waiting for those who have come to a position of maturity where they can handle the things of the Spirit.

Have you come to Jordan? In Jordan, you declare your authority and shout the victory. In Jordan, we do not wake up and cower in fear when the devil comes in the night time; we just tell him, "Get out!" It's another life in Jordan. There, you understand what Jesus meant when He said, "You are not of this world" (John 15:19).

Don't stay at Jericho; move on to Jordan! There's a better life in Jordan. I've seen warriors of Christ who died most miserably. They suffered things they shouldn't have suffered. I've seen people who prophesied, laid hands on the sick and cast out devils, who have not been able to handle life's simplest issues. They couldn't, because they stopped at Jericho. They went to war at Jericho, but they didn't move on to Jordan to understand spiritual authority and the eternal life in Jordan.

Conclusion

"(God) Who hath saved us, and called us with an holy calling, not according to our works, but according to his own purpose and grace, which was given us in Christ Jesus before the world began, But is now made manifest by the appearing of our Saviour Jesus Christ, who hath abolished death, and hath brought life and immortality to light through the gospel:" (2 Timothy1:10).

There's another life, and God has brought it to light, He has revealed it to us through the gospel. This is why He calls us a new breed of people, **"...a chosen generation, a royal priesthood, an holy nation, a peculiar people; that ye should show forth the praises** (the virtues and perfections) **of him who hath called you out of darkness into his marvellous light" (1 Peter 2:9).**

It's our calling, that's why you must refuse to remain in Gilgal. Move on to Bethel, and when you get to Bethel, don't stay there, move on to Jericho! Don't stop at Jericho either; go on to Jordan, for Jordan is the place we have been called to in the New Testament, Hallelujah!

"Blessed be the God and Father of our Lord Jesus Christ, who hath

blessed us with all spiritual blessings in heavenly places in Christ: According as he hath chosen us in him before the foundation of the world, that we should be holy and without blame before him in love: Having predestinated us unto the adoption of children by Jesus Christ to himself, according to the good pleasure of his will," (Ephesians 1:3-5).

This is the adoption we've been talking about, when you are raised and trained by the Father to the stage of maturity, that's when He delivers the world into your hands; and it takes place in Jordan.

"Now I say, That the heir, as long as he is a child, differeth nothing from a servant, though he be lord of all;

But is under tutors and governors until the time appointed of the father" (Galatians 4:1-20).

Notice the Scripture doesn't say until a time the heir appoints by himself, but until a time appointed by his Father. You're already an heir of God, a joint-heir with Christ, but as long as you're a child, you will not be different from a servant. You'll find sometimes that the same things that happen to unbelievers happen to you also. Don't wonder where the problem is, it's because you're still a child! You need to grow.

Paul says the heir is placed under tutors and governors; that's the training process, that's how he is brought up. That's why the Bible lets us know,

"...he gave some, apostles; and some, prophets; and some, evangelists; and some, pastors and teachers; For the perfecting of the saints, for the work of the ministry, for the edifying of the body of Christ: Till we all come in the unity of the faith, and of the knowledge of the Son of God, unto a perfect man, unto the measure of the stature of the fulness of Christ: That we henceforth be no more children, tossed to and fro, and carried about with every wind of doctrine, by the sleight of men, and cunning craftiness, whereby they lie in wait to deceive; But speaking the truth in love, may grow up into him in all things, which is the head, even Christ:" (Ephesians 4:11-13).

It's time for you to grow up in God; it's time to move forward in your walk with the Lord. Get up from Gilgal and move on to Bethel! Now, don't stop at Bethel, move from there to Jericho. But remember, there's a place beyond Jericho – there's a Jordan to get to! So, don't Stop here, move on to Jordan!

To know more about
the ministry and messages of
Pastor Chris Oyakhilome
contact:

CHRIST EMBASSY

aka Believers' LoveWorld Inc.

United Kingdom:

Believers' LoveWorld
Unit C2, Thames view
Business center
Barlow way, Rainham
Essex, RM 13 8BT
Tel: +44 (0) 170 855 6604

South Africa:

303 Pretoria Avenue
Cnr.Harley and Bram Fischer,
Randburg, Gauteng, South Africa.
Tel:+27-11-326 0971,
+27-11-326 0972

Nigeria:

Christ Embassy
Plot 97, Durumi District,
Abuja, Nigeria.
LoveWorld Conference Center
Kudirat Abiola Way, Oregun
P.O. Box 13563 Ikeja, Lagos.
Tel:+234-808 586 5700,
+234-817 198 7339
+234-802 478 9892-3
or email: info@loveworldbooks.org
website: www.loveworldbooks.org

Please include your testimony or help received from this book when you write.

Your prayer requests are also welcome.